Sensational Survivors

An illustrated guide to New Zealand's remarkable wildlife

Sandra Morris

WALKER BOOKS
AND SUBSIDIARIES

LONDON • BOSTON • SYDNEY • AUCKLAND

For the late Geoff Moon – a great friend and mentor to many young New Zealand naturalists – SM

First published in 2010
by Walker Books Australia Pty Ltd
Locked Bag 22, Newtown
NSW 2042 Australia
www.walkerbooks.com.au

The moral rights of the author have been asserted.

Text and illustrations © 2010 Sandra Morris

All rights reserved. No part of this publication may be reproduced, stored in a retrieval system, or transmitted in any form or by any means – electronic, mechanical, photocopying, recording or otherwise – without the prior written permission of the publisher.

National Library of Australia Cataloguing-in-Publication entry:

Morris, Sandra.

Sensational survivors / Sandra Morris.

ISBN: 978 1 921150 66 1 (pbk.)

For primary school age.

Subjects: Animals – New Zealand – Juvenile literature.

591.993

Typeset in Avril and Univers

The illustrations for this book were drawn with graphite pencil and painted with watercolours.
Cover illustrations © Sandra Morris
Cover photographs © iStockphoto.com

Printed and bound in China

10 9 8 7 6 5 4 3 2 1

Contents

ECHOES OF GONDWANA • 4

NEW ARRIVALS • 6

ANCIENT SURVIVORS • 8

GONE FOREVER • 10

A NATIONAL TREASURE • 12

EPIC JOURNEYS • 14

ALL AT SEA • 18

WHAT'S FOR DINNER? • 22

UP ALL NIGHT • 26

LOVE IS IN THE AIR • 29

BRINGING UP THE KIDS • 32

GETTING UNDRESSED • 36

STAYING ALIVE • 38

A HELPING HAND • 42

GLOSSARY • 44

INDEX • 47

ACKNOWLEDGEMENTS AND REFERENCES • 48

Echoes of Gondwana

500 MILLION YEARS AGO
The first fish appear.

400 MILLION YEARS AGO
Marine animals increase. Insects are found.

350 MILLION YEARS AGO
Amphibians move onto dry land. Early land plants evolve. Flying insects are seen.

1.8 MILLION YEARS AGO Humans appear.

20 MILLION YEARS AGO
Volcanic activity causes new mountains to emerge. New Zealand saved from rising seas.

1000 YEARS AGO
First humans arrive in New Zealand.

Did you know that some of the oldest and oddest creatures in the world are found in New Zealand?

New Zealand was once part of an ancient supercontinent, which we call Gondwana. Around 80 million years ago, the mass of land that is now New Zealand drifted away from Gondwana into isolation. Imagine New Zealand as a raft, and its creatures as strange cargo. On board that raft were special creatures that evolved into some of the unusual species living there today. The absence of large mammals made New Zealand a safe haven for the creatures there.

5

New arrivals

Not all of New Zealand's wildlife evolved from these early animal inhabitants. Some species were much later arrivals. And some are the descendants of those that flew or "ocean hopped" from other countries later.

Wind dispersal and "ocean hopping" has continued to bring new species to New Zealand. The **silvereye** in 1856, the **monarch butterfly** in 1873, the **white-faced heron** in the 1940s, the **welcome swallow** in 1958 and more recently, the **spur-winged plover**, all travelled from afar.

Over the years pests, such as rats, cats, ferrets, stoats, weasels and possums, have also been introduced. These pests have preyed on New Zealand's native animals, threatening the survival of some species.

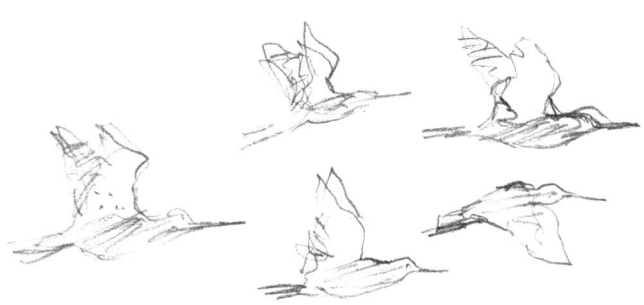

MONARCH BUTTERFLIES FROM NORTH AND SOUTH AMERICA

SILVEREYE FINCHES FROM AUSTRALIA

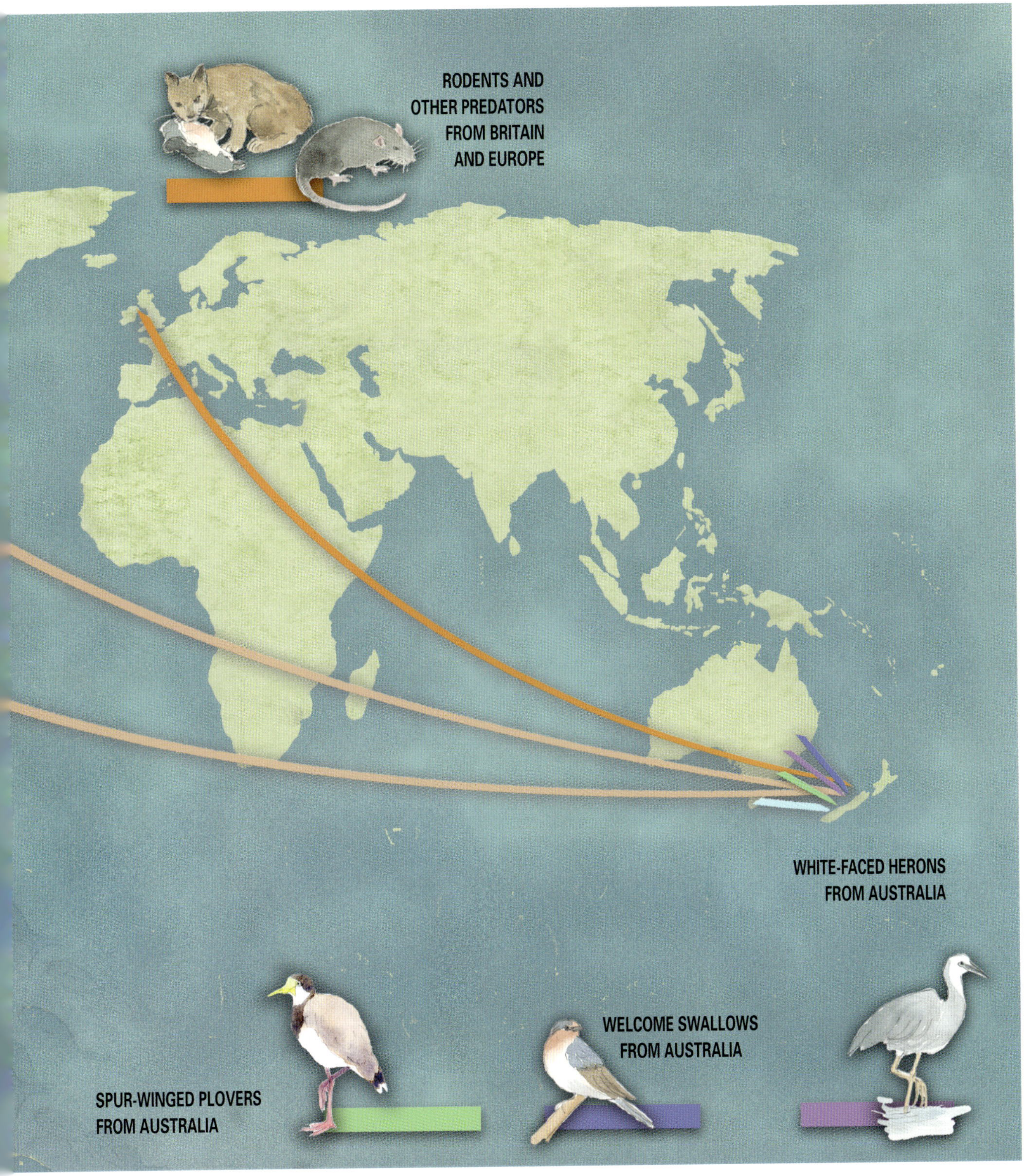

RODENTS AND OTHER PREDATORS FROM BRITAIN AND EUROPE

WHITE-FACED HERONS FROM AUSTRALIA

SPUR-WINGED PLOVERS FROM AUSTRALIA

WELCOME SWALLOWS FROM AUSTRALIA

Ancient survivors

Some of New Zealand's animals set records for survival. The tuatara is the most famous survivor, but a number of other species have scarcely changed from the times of Gondwana to the present.

Tuatara can live up to one hundred years.

Tuatara have been around for more than 225 million years – long before the giant dinosaurs.

They may look like lizards, but they are actually related to another ancient group of reptiles.

They have a "third eye" in the middle of their forehead that has a lens, retina and optic nerve, but it is covered by scales. It is thought the eye may function as a biological clock.

Hamilton's frog is one of four surviving species of primitive native frogs.

Hamilton's frog is one of the rarest frogs in the world. It has been around as long as the tuatara. Unlike most frogs it has very little webbing on its feet and spends its time hiding under plants and rocks where it is damp.

Kauri snails can live for more than 20 years.

Kauri snails have been around for millions of years. These slow-growing creatures can take up to 15 years to mature. Some have shells the size of a human hand.

The **peripatus** has lived for more than 300 million years. There are approximately 30 kinds of peripatus unique to New Zealand and these species are not unlike their ancestors. They come in many different colours.

Peripatus have soft, velvety skin and are often called "velvet worms".

Short-tailed bats are one of the few bats which hunt on the ground.

Short-tailed bats have lived as long as the tuatara. They were the only land mammals in New Zealand when humans arrived. Now they are found at only a handful of sites.

Some giant weta can reach 20 centimetres in total length.

Giant weta have been around since dinosaur times. They are the largest insect in New Zealand, but these "gentle giants" are often shy and hard to find.

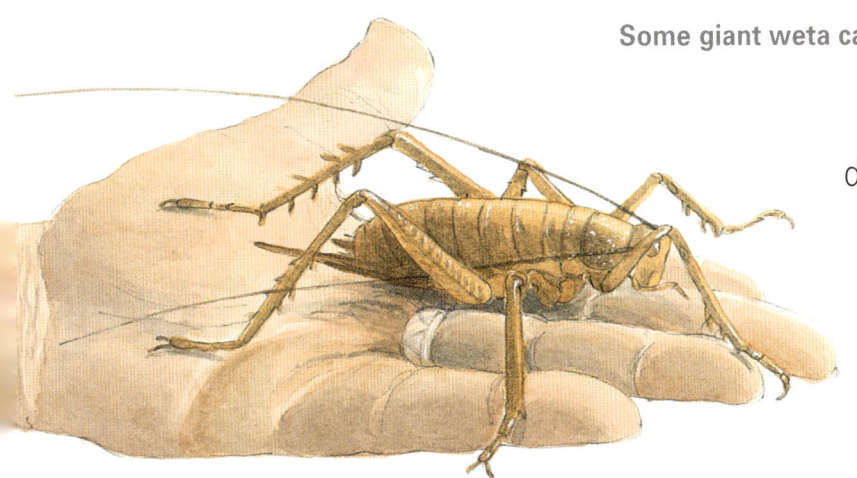

Gone forever

The special traits that New Zealand's creatures developed made them particularly vulnerable to change. When humans arrived, native creatures were no longer safe in their natural habitat. Sadly, some creatures have been lost forever.

The first people to arrive in New Zealand were the Maori. They were superb hunters and also cleared large areas of forest. While the Maori introduced the kiore, a Pacific rat, the Europeans brought even more predatory animals, including other species of rats, cats, ferrets, weasels, dogs and possums, that reminded them of home. And some Europeans hunted the unique creatures – to them, a prize specimen in a museum case meant more than a live animal in the wild. As settlers cleared forest for land, animal habitat was increasingly lost.

Moa could not fly.

Moa were the only birds in the world without wings. There were nine species. The smallest was the coastal moa which stood at 60 centimetres. The largest, the giant moa, reached two metres to the top of its back and was the tallest bird ever to have lived. Giant moa could carry up to five kilograms of stones inside their stomachs for grinding down plant food. Moa probably became extinct by the 14th century.

The laughing owl got its name from its strange loud cry.

The **laughing owl**, or whekau, could be heard at dusk on rainy nights. It roosted and nested in caves and hollow trees. Its strong talons and feet helped it tackle prey such as tuatara, kiwi, ducks and morepork. It was last seen around the early 1900s.

The Haast's eagle was the largest known eagle on Earth.

Known as the "tiger of the skies", the **Haast's eagle** was New Zealand's top predator. With a wingspan of up to three metres and claws as large as a tiger's, it could tackle even the giant moa. It is believed that many New Zealand birds developed drab plumage and became flightless and nocturnal to protect themselves from this monstrous predator. Haast's eagles became extinct through hunting by humans and the loss of their food source.

The **huia** was the only bird species in the world where male and female had very different shaped beaks. The male used his stout bill to tear at wood to search for grubs and beetles, while the female used her long curved bill to dig for grubs. The last huia was seen in 1907.

Huia were the largest of New Zealand's wattle birds.

The world's largest gecko, **Delcourt's gecko**, or kawekaweau, is thought to have lived in New Zealand. A stuffed specimen of a Delcourt's gecko was found in a French museum in 1979, but to date no fossil bones have been found. It became extinct around the early 1800s.

Delcourt's gecko was 62 centimetres long.

The **Stephen's Island wren** was the smallest flightless bird ever to have lived. It scurried around the undergrowth in search of food. The lighthouse keeper on Stephen's Island was the only European to see the wren. Unfortunately, in 1894, his cat hunted the very last one.

The Stephen's Island wren belonged to the most ancient group of perching birds.

11

A national treasure

The kiwi is special, as it behaves more like a mammal than a bird. It is so special, it has become a national icon. It is seen on stamps, coins and as a symbol for locally made products. New Zealanders even call themselves kiwis!

There are two groups of **kiwi**: the **brown kiwi** and the **spotted kiwi**.

Brown kiwi have three species: the North Island brown, the rowi and the tokoeka.

There are two kinds of spotted kiwi: the little spotted and the great spotted.

Kiwi belong to the same family of flightless birds as the extinct moa. Their closest relatives, however, are Australian cassowaries and emus. Kiwi have tiny wings but they cannot fly. Instead, they can run fast over long distances – they can even outrun humans. And their claws can be lethal weapons.

In the early 1900s there were approximately 12 million kiwi in New Zealand – now there are around 75 000.

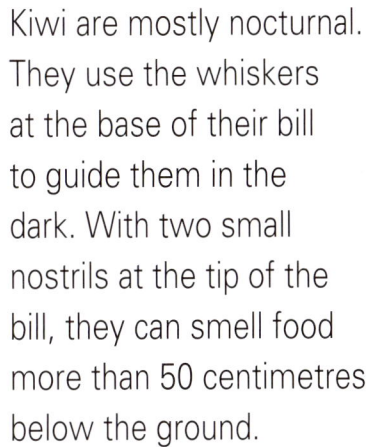

Kiwi are mostly nocturnal. They use the whiskers at the base of their bill to guide them in the dark. With two small nostrils at the tip of the bill, they can smell food more than 50 centimetres below the ground.

Unlike most birds, kiwi create burrows rather than nests. One pair of kiwi can have many burrows covering territory as large as 60 football fields!

The kiwi is the only bird which has nostrils at the tip of its bill.

Compared to her body size, the female kiwi lays one of the biggest eggs around. A kiwi egg weighs the same as six hens' eggs. Carrying such a huge egg is not easy. The female kiwi will often stand in water to relieve her aching legs.

During her lifetime, a female can lay up to 100 eggs.

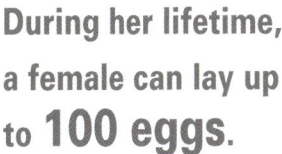

Once the egg has been laid in the burrow, the male kiwi incubates it for two and a half months. Kiwi chicks don't have an egg tooth to help them break out of their shells – instead they peck and kick their way out with their legs. Their yolk sac keeps them nourished for up to a week.

Epic journeys

Animals travel for all sorts of reasons, some to breed, some in the search for food. New Zealand boasts many record-breaking animal travellers.

Humpback whales, or paikea, migrate from their breeding grounds in Tonga, via New Zealand's waters, to Antarctica where they dine on massive quantities of krill. They are slow swimmers, travelling as little as six to twelve kilometres an hour.

Many Maori believe whales are their guardians and that they escorted some of their ancestral canoes. In Maori stories, Paikea, a very important ancestor, arrived in New Zealand from Hawaiki on the back of a whale.

Bar-tailed godwits fly nonstop from Alaska to New Zealand to feed on the mudflats during the Southern Hemisphere summer. This is the longest nonstop flight known for any bird. The godwits double their body weight for the return flight to the Alaskan tundra for breeding.

Humpback whales have the longest migration of any mammal.

Royal albatross, or toroa, have wings that are long and narrow – specially suited to gliding. They can glide up to 140 kilometres per hour, often without a single wing beat. This is called "dynamic soaring".

Royal albatross spend nearly 90 per cent of their lives at sea making long migratory flights around the Southern Ocean.

In its lifetime the godwit can fly further than from Earth to the moon.

About 100 000 bar-tailed godwits journey to New Zealand each year.

Royal albatross are among the largest seabirds in the world.

15

The yellow-eyed penguin is one of the world's rarest penguins.

Yellow-eyed penguins, or hoiho, travel up to 30 kilometres from the shore in search of food. They move their flippers underwater as though they are flying.

Like porpoises, they surface and dive in and out of the water so they can continue to breathe. They can reach speeds of up to 12 kilometres per hour.

The Maori name for yellow-eyed penguins, **hoiho, means "noise shouter"** and when the penguins arrive on shore it's easy to understand why!

Kauri snails prefer moist conditions.

On a wet night **kauri snails,** or pupu rangi, can travel up to 200 metres. This may not seem like far, but it would be like a human walking for two kilometres just to go to the corner shop.

The female kakapo can be away from the nest for several hours.

The female **kakapo** is a hard-working solo mother. She walks many kilometres each night looking for food for her growing chicks.

Crayfish walk along the sea floor against the current.

Crayfish are capable of marching huge distances for breeding. Some red rock crayfish can travel up to six kilometres in a day, and move as far as 460 kilometres for their annual migration. Packhorse crayfish have been known to travel 1070 kilometres.

New Zealand long-finned eels, whose Maori name is tuna, live in rivers, lakes or wetlands for most of their lives. Then, after many years, they migrate 5000 kilometres to the South Pacific near Tonga to breed. Soon after laying their eggs, they die. The fertilised eggs or larvae float on ocean currents for about 15 months. When they reach New Zealand they change into transparent "glass" eels and travel inland up rivers, changing yet again into elvers before becoming adult eels.

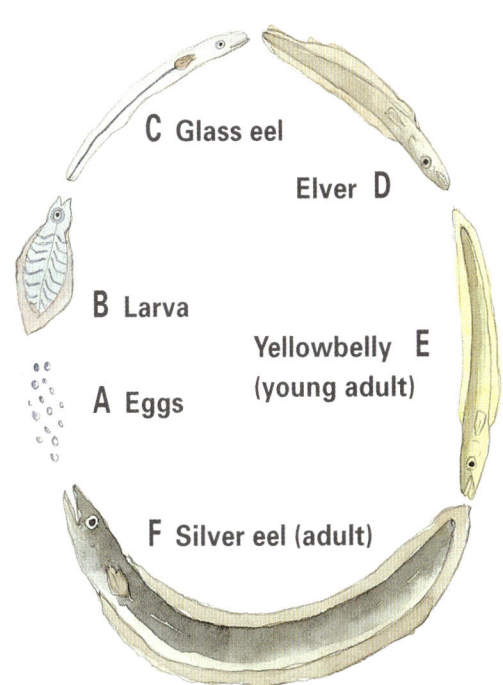

All at sea

A long coastline and vast oceans make New Zealand's marine life unusually rich.

Fur seals spend a lot of their time on rocky shores.

New Zealand sea lions are also known as Hooker's sea lions.

Fur seals, or kekeno, have two layers of fur for insulation to keep their bodies warm and dry while at sea. They are excellent swimmers – some New Zealand fur seals even make their way to Australia!

Weaned **fur seal pups** have been found **more than 1000 kilometres from their birthplace.**

New Zealand sea lions, or rapoka, can dive as deep as 600 metres, staying under water for up to 13 minutes. When diving deeply their heart rate drops to only four to six beats per minute to conserve oxygen.

A dominant male elephant seal can have between 25 and 50 females in his "harem".

Male **elephant seals**, or ihupuku, are the largest seals in the world – and the deepest divers. They can hold their breath for over an hour under water.

Elephant seals may be awkward on land, but they are excellent at swimming and diving.

Hector's and **Maui's dolphins** are among the rarest dolphins in the world – with 7000–8000 Hector's off the South Island and just over 100 Maui's left off the North Island. Hector's dolphins, or upokohue, are also the smallest dolphins. They are the only dolphins in New Zealand with a rounded black dorsal fin. All other dolphins have a pointy fin like a shark.

Hector's dolphins are only found in New Zealand waters.

Albatross spend most of their lives at sea.

After leaving the nest young **albatross** do not return to land for three to five years. In this time they sleep on the wing and rest on the water. When they finally do come back to shore they stagger about as their tender feet are not strong enough to support their bodies.

When orca sleep only half the brain shuts down and the other half stays alert while the orca listens out for danger.

Orca, or maki, are sometimes called killer whales, but they are actually the largest member of the dolphin family. They are fierce hunters, although there are no known cases of these creatures ever killing humans in the wild.

Each **humpback whale** has a unique pattern on the edge of its tail flukes so it can be easily identified – a bit like a human fingerprint.

Humpback whales often slap their flukes against the water. This is called lobtailing.

Giant squid breed in deep waters around New Zealand.

The **giant squid** lives at depths of 300–600 metres. The world's largest invertebrate, it grows at an average rate of three centimetres per day, reaching a massive length of 12 metres in 12–18 months.

Giant squid can weigh as much as 275 kilograms.

Nudibranchs are known as "butterflies of the sea", as they come in a variety of shapes and colours.

The most common nudibranch in New Zealand waters is the **clown nudibranch**. Its bright colours warn fish that it is poisonous and what look like purple feathers on its back are really gills for breathing.

Some nudibranchs are **great thieves**. When a nudibranch **eats another creature** that has stinging cells, the nudibranch incorporates the **stingers** into its own system and uses them as protection against predators.

What's for dinner?

Finding food is an all-important task for most species, and creatures can go about this in surprisingly different ways.

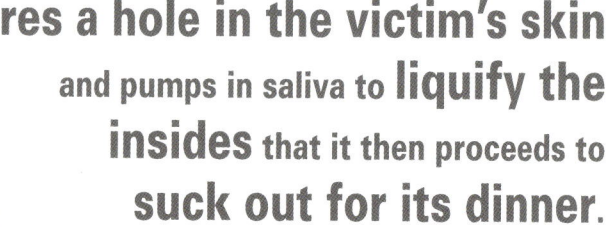

The **peripatus** fires out a net of sticky glue-like saliva to catch its prey. **It bores a hole in the victim's skin** and pumps in saliva to **liquify the insides** that it then proceeds to **suck out for its dinner**.

Peripatus recognise prey such as spiders, cockroaches and weta with their sensitive antennae.

Kauri snails are carnivorous – they eat live earthworms which they suck up like spaghetti. The insides of their mouths are lined with rows and rows of hundreds of small, sharp teeth that grind off bits of food.

Kauri snails eat earthworms, insects and even other snails.

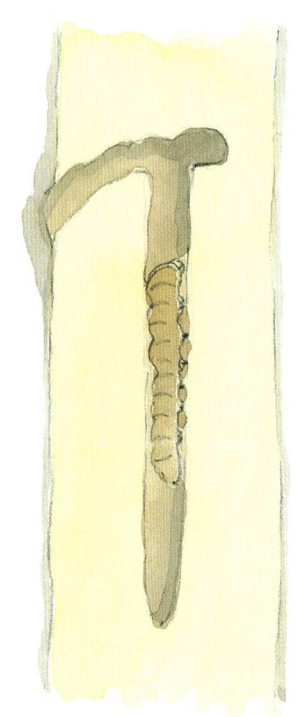

Puriri caterpillars burrow deep inside trees, feeding on the wood with their powerful jaws. When they become moths they do not have mouth parts or digestive systems so they cannot eat.

Puriri caterpillars feed on tissue inside trees such as the titoki, the putaputaweta and the puriri, from which they get their name.

Kea are opportunists. They eat a wide variety of food, tasting it with their tongues before eating. They need a lot of body fat to survive the freezing conditions of the South Island, so sometimes they attack sheep for fat and protein. They often use their strong beaks to scavenge food from rubbish bins around ski fields.

Kea are good at finding fatty foods, such as margarine from discarded containers.

Tui are honeyeaters, feeding mostly on nectar from native plants. They have brush-tipped tongues to reach the nectar. Maori taught young male birds to recite up to 50 words.

The **wood pigeon**, or kereru, is New Zealand's biggest forest bird and eats the fruit of trees such as miro, tawa and karaka. It is an important part of the ecological balance as it is the only bird capable of eating the larger native fruits. When the seeds pass through the bird, they are "planted" through the forest complete with their own pile of manure, soon to grow into new trees.

Tui will travel long distances for favourite plant nectars.

Wood pigeons help to regenerate New Zealand's forests.

Humpback whales can eat more than 1000 kilograms of food in a day!

Humpback whales blow a cloud of bubbles around their prey like a net and gulp in water along with the fish. They filter the water out of their mouths, leaving the fish inside.

Open wide: the jaws of the **albatross** are hinged well back in its head so it can open its bill wide enough to swallow large catches such as squid and octopus.

However, **dinner must taste very dull**, as the albatross has only one hundred taste buds compared to our nine thousand! Albatross eat some fish, **but their favourite meal is squid**.

Short-tailed bats have adapted to hunt on the forest floor.

Unlike most bats that catch their prey in the air, **short-tailed bats** forage on the ground for insects. They are also attracted to the native wood rose. The bats use their brush-tipped tongues to soak up its nectar – a bit like a paintbrush with water.

While most ducks are vegetarian, **blue ducks**, or whio, eat insects. They scrape off the larvae of aquatic insects from rocks with their specially designed bills. The soft flesh on the tip of the bill protects it from constant scraping.

Blue ducks have large webbed feet so they can feed in rapid-moving water.

Up all night

Many of New Zealand's creatures wake as night falls. Some even have special adaptations for finding their way in the dark.

The **puriri moth** is the largest moth in New Zealand and is found only on the North Island. The female has a wingspan of nearly 15 centimetres. Adults emerge from holes in trees on warm, humid nights. They live only a few nights – enough time to mate and lay eggs.

The puriri moth is sometimes known as the ghost moth because its pale green wings look ghostly in the moonlight.

During the day **giant weta** hide under rocks and bark and in the foliage of trees. They come out at night to feed mainly on leaves.

In Maori stories weta were called "taipo" which means "devils of the night".

Maori stories referred to short-tailed and long-tailed bats as "pekapeka".
It was believed the bats came from the underworld and were bad luck as they came out at night.

Short-tailed bats are one of only two native land mammals in New Zealand. They only emerge at night but cannot see well in the dark. Instead, the bats send out high-pitched sounds that bounce off objects giving them information about what's nearby. Unlike other bats they scamper on the ground using their folded wings as front legs, and their wrists as feet.

Brown geckos can be pollinators.

All **brown geckos** in New Zealand are nocturnal, while all **green geckos** are active during the day.

Brown geckos feed on the nectar of flowers, such as those found on pohutukawa trees. The pollen that rubs off on their throats and chins is transferred to other pohutukawa trees, fertilising them as they visit.

Moreporks, or ruru, hunt silently at night when most other birds are asleep. The tips of their wing feathers are very soft and make no sound as they fly so they can surprise their prey.

Moreporks are New Zealand's only surviving native owls.

Kakapo means night parrot. It is the world's heaviest parrot. It is also the world's only flightless nocturnal parrot. The whiskers around its face help it find its way at night.

The kakapo **weighs as much as a newborn baby**.

Kakapo cannot fly but they are good climbers.

Love is in the air

Finding a mate is the essential first step to rearing a family. To pair up, many creatures show off to potential partners. The signals they send out vary widely.

Spotted shags, or parekareka, know how to stand out in breeding season. They grow a headdress of black crests, their dark brown eyes are ringed with blue "eye shadow" and the skin around their bill becomes a vivid green. Their yellow feet complete the outfit.

Spotted shags lose their black crest and bright colours once the breeding season is over.

To call to females, the male **tree weta** makes a rasping sound by rubbing its legs against its body. This is known as "stridulation".

Weta can vary the rasping sounds they make to send different messages.

29

Kauri snails mate when it rains.

New Zealand's native **kauri snails** are hermaphrodites – each kauri snail is both male and female – but their eggs still need to be fertilised by another snail.

The snails lay their eggs through a hole in their neck!

Wood pigeons' stunning aerial displays are called "stunting".

In spring male **wood pigeons** show off to the females with spectacular flying displays. They swoop up out of the forest high in the air, stall and then plummet back down to the trees, then swoop back up again.

The male kakapo's call can travel up to five kilometres.

During the breeding season the male **kakapo** puts on a real show. First he clears away debris for a stage. Then he puffs himself up like a balloon and makes booming calls that resonate out over the bushland and valleys. When the females arrive at the site, sometimes the male will perform a wing-waving dance. Each male tries to outperform the other. The best male wins the female.

Each year male humpback whales produce a new song.

Male **humpback whales** often "serenade" the females. They sing haunting, complex songs for up to 30 minutes at a time and can go on for hours reaching other whales as far as 160 kilometres away. When the whales surface to breathe they start their songs from the beginning.

Bringing up the kids

Most animals take great care of their young and try to make homes in safe places protected from predators. Some parents share the rearing of the young, while for others it's either the male or the female that does the caring.

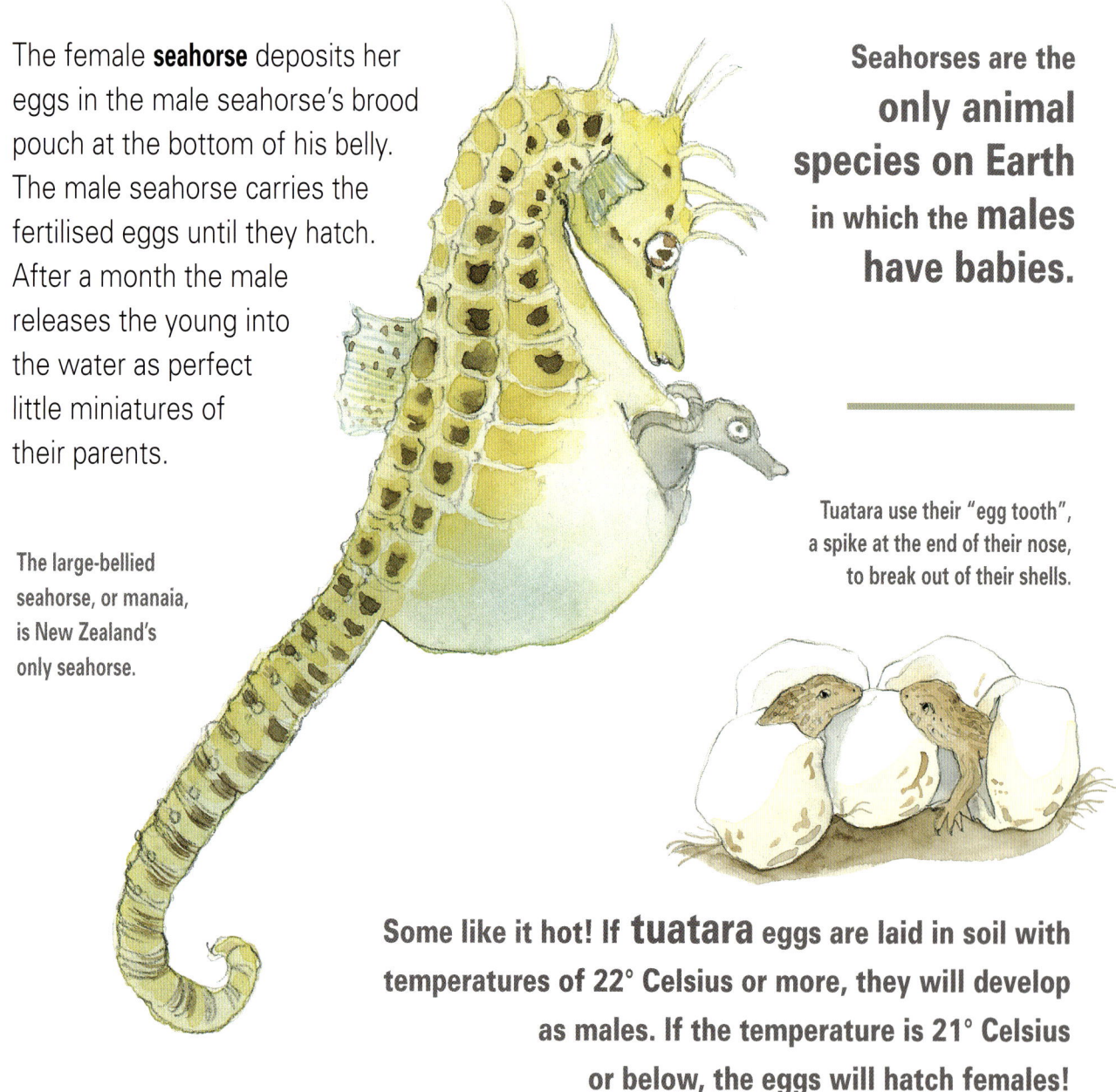

The female **seahorse** deposits her eggs in the male seahorse's brood pouch at the bottom of his belly. The male seahorse carries the fertilised eggs until they hatch. After a month the male releases the young into the water as perfect little miniatures of their parents.

The large-bellied seahorse, or manaia, is New Zealand's only seahorse.

Seahorses are the **only animal species on Earth** in which the **males have babies.**

Tuatara use their "egg tooth", a spike at the end of their nose, to break out of their shells.

Some like it hot! If **tuatara** eggs are laid in soil with temperatures of 22° Celsius or more, they will develop as males. If the temperature is 21° Celsius or below, the eggs will hatch females!

The kingfisher, or kotare, hammers its bill into rotten trees and clay banks to make nesting holes.

Kingfisher parents are poor housekeepers. Their nest soon becomes a mess of rotten food and droppings. It's quite easy to find such a loud, smelly nest but cleverly, the chicks are safely hidden at the end of a long tunnel.

The male **Archey's frog** fertilises and protects the eggs laid by the female. When the young tailed froglets hatch they wriggle up onto their father's back for three to four weeks while they grow stronger.

Unlike other frogs, the tadpole stage for the Archey's frog takes place in the egg.

33

The sticky pink ribbon of eggs laid by the nudibranch, **Jason mirabilis**, attach to its host hydroid plant.

Sometimes it can take up to 13 hours to lay the eggs and there can be up to **78 000 eggs** in a single strand!

Most nudibranchs have colour-coordinated egg ribbons that perfectly match their body colour.

Long-tailed cuckoos, or koekoea, are not nest builders. Instead, they take over the nest of the whitehead. They throw out the whitehead eggs and lay their own eggs in the nest, leaving the little whitehead to do all the work.

Young long-tailed cuckoos can even mimic the call of whitehead chicks.

The wrybill's grey-blue eggs are camouflaged by the stones.

The **wrybill**, or ngutu-parore, lays two eggs amongst the stones on rocky South Island riverbeds. It builds its nest on shingle "islands" in the rivers, safe from stoats, cats and rats.

Unlike other geckos that lay eggs, **New Zealand geckos** give birth to live young. This is an adaptation to New Zealand's cooler summer temperatures. When they give birth, New Zealand geckos nearly always have twins!

The only other geckos that can give birth to live young are in New Caledonia but they also sometimes lay eggs depending on the temperature.

Getting undressed

Growing up for some animals means changing outfits. Their skins don't grow with them so they need to shed their old ones. Some creatures can do this many times in their lives, but for others it's a one-time performance.

With all the swimming and diving in salty seas, the **yellow-eyed penguin**'s feathers wear out and must be replaced. It takes three to four weeks to shed and regrow its feathers. During this time, the penguin cannot go to sea to feed, so it must find a safe, quiet place to rest.

The penguins lose up to four kilograms in body weight during the moult.

Elephant seals are almost hairless. They moult once a year, their skin falling off in big patches.

Like the yellow-eyed penguins, elephant seals do not go into the water while moulting.

Peripatus shed their skin like peeling off a sock.

Peripatus shed their outer skin every few weeks to allow growth.

A cicada, or kikihi, and its empty nymphal skin.

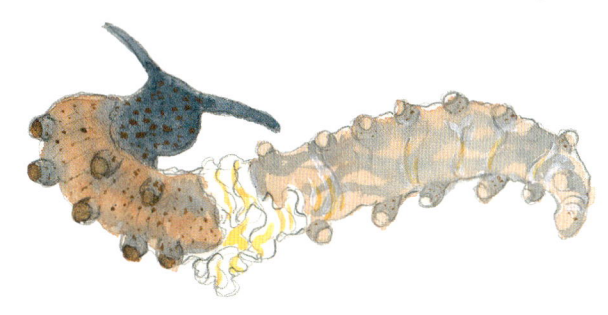

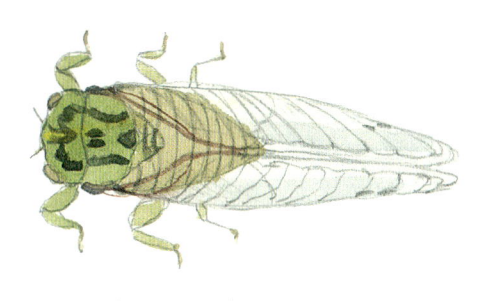

When **weta** moult they split their exoskeletons and wriggle out. They **eat the old skin** for nourishing protein.

Weta moult about nine times in their lives.

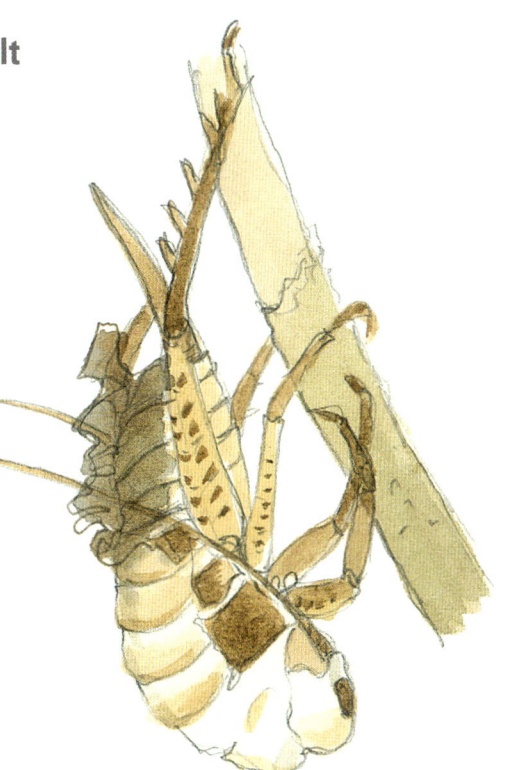

Cicada larvae spend their time underground. After many years the adult cicadas emerge and shed their "nymphal" skins, revealing wings underneath. If you look around trees in spring, you might find some of their discarded skins clinging to the bark.

A gecko even sheds the skin over its eyes.

As it grows, a **gecko**'s skin doesn't grow with it so it moults. Sometimes the gecko leaves behind a complete inside-out gecko skin.

Staying alive

New Zealand's animals have developed some clever tactics to protect their territory – and to avoid being eaten. Some fly or run away, others put up a fight, and some hide, using camouflage to blend in with their surroundings.

Female tusked weta do not have tusks.

Male **tusked weta** defend their territory from rival males by using their tusks. They lock their heads together with their tusks and push with their back legs. The first one to fall over is the loser.

Tree weta and giant weta hold up two legs when threatened.

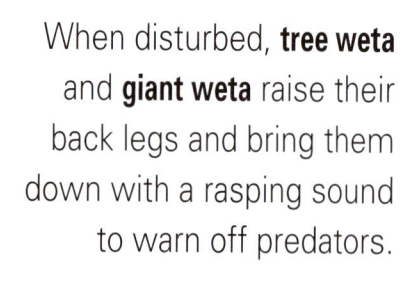

When disturbed, **tree weta** and **giant weta** raise their back legs and bring them down with a rasping sound to warn off predators.

The **spikes** along the weta's legs could **easily damage a bird's eye.**

The egg-laying skink stays close to the shoreline.

The **egg-laying skink** hides its eggs under rocks on the beach. When disturbed on land it plunges into rock pools to escape danger.

Some skinks will stay underwater for twenty minutes!

The Australasian bittern lives in densely vegetated wetlands.

Camouflaged feathers and a swaying movement make the **Australasian bittern**, or matuku, hard to spot against the moving reeds.

When threatened, the Australasian bittern will point its bill skywards and "freeze".

To protect its young, the New Zealand dotterel puts on a broken wing act.

When a predator approaches a **New Zealand dotterel**, or tuturiwhatu, in its nest, the adult bird will lure the predator away from the nest by pretending to have a broken wing. It will call out repeatedly to the predator to draw it away from the young.

Unlike most short-horned grasshoppers around the world, "Skiing Siggy" is well adapted to the snowy conditions of its alpine home. This **hairy grasshopper**, or *Sigaus villosus*, gets its nickname from its very agile method of escape from predators. Using its legs as ski poles, it skis on its abdomen down the slopes to escape danger.

The hairy grasshopper is the largest alpine grasshopper in New Zealand and lives at higher altitudes than other grasshoppers.

Brown geckos can drop a tail if attacked and will grow a new one. Each new tail will look a little different.

Unlike brown geckos, green geckos do not shed their tails so easily as they use them as a fifth limb for climbing.

If its nest is in danger, the adult **takahe** buries its beak into the nest to hide its bright red colour.

With only four official sightings between 1800 and 1900, by 1930 takahe were thought to be extinct. Then in 1948, a colony of 250 was found.

41

A helping hand

Sadly, many of New Zealand's animals have become extinct. But there have been some conservation success stories too, such as that of the black robin.

In 1979 the **black robin** was the rarest bird in the world: there were only five remaining black robins, which lived in the Chatham Islands. During the breeding season wildlife officers took black robin eggs from their nests. They placed the eggs in the nests of another bird, the Chatham Island tomtit, where the chicks were hatched and fed until they were two weeks old. Then they took the chicks back to their parents, who had already laid more eggs ready to be transferred. One black robin, Old Blue, lived and bred for 13 years – longer than any other black robin. There are now more than 140 black robins and they are all descended from Old Blue.

Wildlife workers help save some threatened species by breeding them in captivity. Once the animals are able to fend for themselves, they are released back into safe areas in the wild. Island sanctuaries have also been created to allow animals to flourish in isolation. One such island sanctuary is Tiritiri Matangi Island, which is now home to the North Island saddleback, takahe, tuatara and gecko, and many other creatures. Sanctuaries have been built on the mainland too, such as the one in Karori in Wellington, where you'll find little spotted kiwi and kaka, among others!

Here are some things that you can do to help protect New Zealand's sensational survivors:

- When walking, stay on the tracks. The forest floor is home to small animals, such as the weta and peripatus. Watch where you walk on the beach. Birds, such as the New Zealand dotterel and fairy tern, nest on the sand.

- If you see a nest, don't handle eggs or chicks. Move on quickly so the parent bird can return to the nest and keep the eggs or chicks warm.

- Don't litter. Rubbish often ends up in the ocean, endangering marine animals, such as Hector's and Maui's dolphins.

- Keep your dog on a leash, especially in nesting areas. Put a bell on your cat's collar so birds can hear it coming.

- Help protect the yellow-eyed penguin: keep out of fenced-off areas near penguin breeding grounds.

- If you see a sick or stranded animal, contact the wildlife authorities.

When you see an animal, observe it from a distance. **Stay still and quiet** so as not to frighten it.

43

Glossary

ADAPTATION: An adjustment in the physical structure or behaviour of a plant or animal to survive in its environment.

ALPINE: Mountain areas of very high altitudes.

BIOLOGICAL CLOCK: An animal's or human's "internal" clock. For example, our biological clock wakes us to tell us it's daytime and we should be getting out of bed.

BURROW: A hole dug by an animal, such as the kiwi, for shelter and refuge.

CAMOUFLAGE: A colour or pattern on skin, scales, feathers or leaves that helps an animal or plant to blend into the background.

CARNIVOROUS: Flesh-eating; describes an animal that feeds mostly on other animals.

EGG TOOTH: A bony tip of the beak of a bird or the upper jaw of a lizard that helps it chip its way out of an egg when hatching.

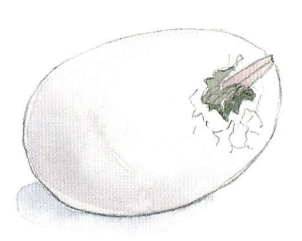

ELVER: A baby eel.

EXOSKELETON: An external skeleton or protective covering, such as the shell of a crustacean.

EXTINCT: Describes a plant or animal species that has died out.

FERTILISE (of plants): When pollen is transferred to a flower from another flower of the same species, leading to the formation of new seeds.

GLASS EEL: The stage of development of an eel between larva and elver (baby eel). The glass eel is transparent, has no teeth and drifts on currents until it is swept into estuaries and there grows into an elver, then eventually, into a mature eel.

GONDWANA: The name we give the ancient supercontinent that existed before Antarctica, New Zealand, Australia, India and parts of Africa and South America split apart to form separate landmasses.

HABITAT: The native area or climate where an animal, bird or plant naturally lives. For example, an eel's natural habitat is a river or pond.

HERMAPHRODITE: Being both male and female at once.

HYDROID: A plant-like creature that protects itself with stinging cells on its tiny tentacles. Closely related to jellyfish.

INCUBATE: To keep eggs warm until they hatch.

KARAKA (tree): A leafy tree growing to about 15 metres. Its yellow fruit is bitter and the fresh kernels are highly toxic.

KRILL: A family of shrimp-like crustaceans, mainly living in huge swarms in Antarctic waters. They are a major food source for whales.

LANDMASS: A body of land, such as a large island or continent, surrounded by water.

LARVA / LARVAE (plural): The young of insects that later develop into other forms, such as caterpillars, butterflies, moths and worms.

MAMMAL: An animal that feeds on milk from its mother.

MIGRATE (verb): To move from one place to another, often to feed or breed.

MIGRATION (noun): The movement from one place to another.

MIRO (tree): A common forest tree growing to around 30 metres at its tallest. Its height is greater the further north it grows.

MOULT: To shed feathers, fur, scales or skin.

NOCTURNAL (adjective): Waking at night and sleeping in the daytime.

NORTH ISLAND: The large northern island of New Zealand.

NUDIBRANCH: A family of marine molluscs (snails) with either no shell, or a very tiny one. They are frequently called "sea slugs", although they are not. Nudibranchs are often brilliantly coloured.

NYMPH (noun): A tiny young insect that hatches in the same form in which it will remain as it grows into adulthood. These insects do not begin as larvae (see Larva / larvae above).

NYMPHAL (adjective): Describes the stage of being a nymph.

OCEAN HOPPING: Animals that move from one piece of land to another, often travelling over large expanses of ocean, sometimes by rafting (travelling aboard a log or floating object).

OPPORTUNISTS: Animals or birds that scavenge for food and will eat almost anything.

PERCHING BIRDS: The name given to the largest family of birds – accounting for 60 per cent of all birds. They all have in common three forward-pointing toes, and one backward. This helps them to balance safely while they roost.

PEST: Animal pests, such as rats and cats, are often introduced and threaten native species and ecosystems.

PLUMAGE: Feathers.

POHUTUKAWA (tree): A red-flowering relative of the myrtle tree. It commonly grows on shorelines and lake edges and is often seen clinging to steep cliffs.

PREDATOR: The animal that hunts another for its food.

PREY: Animals eaten by other animals.

PURIRI (tree): A large, flowering tree popular with birds for its delicious nectar.

PUTAPUTAWETA (tree): A small flowering tree with tiny black fruit.

ROOST (of birds): To sit or rest, often on a branch.

SOUTH ISLAND: The large southern island of New Zealand.

STRIDULATION: The act of producing a sound by rubbing together certain body parts. A weta calls to females using stridulation.

STUNTING: A display of skill or strength. One such example is a wood pigeon's aerial displays.

TALON(s): Claw(s).

TAWA (tree): A large tree with fruit of two to 3.5 centimetres in length. Only the wood pigeon is large enough to swallow and digest the fruit whole without injury.

TERRITORY: The area a creature treats as its own home ground.

TITOKI (tree): A medium-sized tree whose flowers in late summer are followed by red berries.

TUNDRA(s): Huge treeless plains in the Arctic regions of the Northern Hemisphere.

WATTLE (of birds): A coloured fleshy lobe hanging from the bird's face.

WEBBING: A membrane or fold of skin connecting the toes of certain animals, often frogs and ducks.

WETLAND: A swamp or marsh, often the habitat of many frogs and wading birds.

WIND DISPERSAL: Seeds distributed by wind.

WINGSPAN: The measurement of an animal's wings from tip to tip.

YOLK SAC: The part of an egg that the baby bird feeds off before hatching. Most yolks occupy 30 to 45 per cent of the egg. The yolk of the huge kiwi egg is around 65 per cent and can sustain the baby kiwi for a week after hatching.

Index

a
albatross 20, 24
albatross, royal 15
alpine grasshopper 40
Archey's frog 33
Australasian bittern 39
Australian cassowary 12

b
bar-tailed godwit 14, 15
bat 4, 9
bat, long-tailed 27
bat, short-tailed 4, 9, 25, 27
beetle 11
bird 4, 38, 43
bird, forest 23
bittern, Australasian 39
black robin 42
blue duck 25
brown gecko 27, 41
brown kiwi 12
butterfly, monarch 6

c
cassowary, Australian 12
cat 6, 10, 11, 35, 43
caterpillar, puriri 22
Chatham Island tomtit 42
cicada 37
clown nudibranch 21
coastal moa 10
cockroach 22
crayfish 17
crayfish, packhorse 17
crayfish, red rock 17
cuckoo, long-tailed 34

d
Delcourt's gecko 11
dinosaur 4, 8, 9
dog 10, 43
dolphin 4, 20
dolphin, Hector's 19, 43
dolphin, Maui's 19, 43
dotterel, New Zealand 40, 43
duck 10, 25
duck, blue 25

e
eagle, Haast's 11
earthworm 22
eel, New Zealand long-finned 17
egg-laying skink 39
elephant seal 19, 36
emu 12

f
fairy tern 43
ferret 6, 10
fish 5, 21, 24
flying insect 5
forest bird 23
frog, Archey's 33
frog, Hamilton's 8
frog, native 4, 8
fur seal 18

g
gecko 11, 35, 37, 43
gecko, brown 27, 41
gecko, Delcourt's 11
gecko, green 27, 41
gecko, New Zealand 35
giant moa 10, 11
giant squid 21
giant weta 4, 9, 26, 38
godwit, bar-tailed 14, 15
grasshopper, alpine 40
grasshopper, hairy 40
great spotted kiwi 12
green gecko 27, 41
grub 11

h
Haast's eagle 11
hairy grasshopper 40
Hamilton's frog 8
Hector's dolphin 19, 43
heron, white-faced 6, 7
Hooker's sea lion 18
huia 11
humpback whale 14, 20, 24, 31

i
insect 4, 5, 9, 22, 25
insect, flying 5

j
Jason mirabilis nudibranch 34

k
kaka 43
kakapo 16, 28, 30
kauri snail 4, 9, 16, 22, 30
kea 23
kingfisher 33
kiore 10
kiwi 10, 12, 13
kiwi, brown 12
kiwi, spotted 12, 43
krill 14

l
large-bellied seahorse 32
laughing owl 10
little spotted kiwi 12, 43
long-tailed bat 27
long-tailed cuckoo 34

m
Maui's dolphin 19, 43
moa 4, 10, 12
moa, coastal 10
moa, giant 10, 11
monarch butterfly 6
morepork 10, 28
moth, puriri 22, 26

n
native frog 4, 8
native owl 28
New Zealand dotterel 40, 43
New Zealand gecko 35
New Zealand long-finned eel 17
New Zealand sea lion 18
North Island brown kiwi 12
North Island saddleback 43
nudibranch 21, 34
nudibranch, clown 21
nudibranch, Jason mirabilis 34

o
octopus 24
orca 20
owl, laughing 10
owl, native 28

p
Pacific rat 10
packhorse crayfish 17
parrot 28
penguin 4, 43
penguin, yellow-eyed 16, 36, 43
peripatus 9, 22, 37, 43
pigeon, wood 23, 30
porpoise 16
possum 6, 10
puriri caterpillar 22
puriri moth 22, 26

q

r
rat 6, 7, 10, 35
rat, Pacific 10
red rock crayfish 17
robin, black 42
rowi 12
royal albatross 15

s
saddleback, North Island 43
sea lion, Hooker's 18
sea lion, New Zealand 18
seahorse 32
seahorse, large-bellied 32
seal, elephant 19, 36
seal, fur 18
shag, spotted 29
sheep 23
short-tailed bat 4, 9, 25, 27
silvereye 6
skink, egg-laying 39
snail 22
snail, kauri 4, 9, 16, 22, 30
spider 22
spotted kiwi 12, 43
spotted shag 29
spur-winged plover 6, 7
squid 24
squid, giant 21
Stephen's Island wren 11
stoat 6, 35
swallow, welcome 6, 7

t
takahe 41, 43
tern, fairy 43
tokoeka 12
tomtit, Chatham Island 42
tree weta 29, 38
tuatara 8, 9, 10, 32, 43
tui 23
tusked weta 38

u, v

w
wattle bird 11
weasel 6, 10
welcome swallow 6, 7
weta 22, 26, 29, 37, 43
weta, giant 4, 9, 26, 38
weta, tree 29, 38
weta, tusked 38
whale 4
whale, humpback 14, 20, 24, 31
white-faced heron 6, 7
whitehead 34
wood pigeon 23, 30
wren, Stephen's Island 11
wrybill 35

x

y
yellow-eyed penguin 16, 36, 43

z

Acknowledgements

I would like to thank the scientists and photographers who helped with this book – especially Rod Morris and Brian Gill. Thanks also to Sarah Matthewson for her contribution with the original text. Special thanks to the hardworking creative team at Walker Books Australia – Sarah Foster, Donna Rawlins, Virginia Grant and Jessica Owen.

References

If you want to find out more about New Zealand's fascinating creatures, look for the following books:

Hunt, Janet and Lucas, Rob,
From Weta to Kauri,
Random House, New Zealand, 2004

Hutching, Gerard,
The Penguin Natural World of New Zealand,
Penguin, New Zealand, 2004

Lindsey, Terence and Morris, Rod,
Collins Field Guide to New Zealand Wildlife,
HarperCollins, New Zealand, 2000

Morris, Rod and Ballance, Alison,
Rare Wildlife of New Zealand,
Random House, New Zealand, 2008

Orbell, Margaret,
The Natural World of the Maori,
Collins/Bateman, New Zealand, 1985

Stace, Glenys and Eagle, Mike,
Yes! We had Dinosaurs,
Penguin, New Zealand, 2001

Tennyson, Alan and Martinson, Paul,
Extinct Birds of New Zealand,
Te Papa Press, 2006

You'll also find many helpful internet sites, including:

Kiwi Conservation Club
www.kcc.org.nz

Department of Conservation
www.doc.govt.nz/conservation